About the Author

Uditha Bandara is specializes in Game development for Windows Phone, Xbox 360, PC, and Zune. He is the South East Asia's First XNA/DirectX MVP (Most Valuable Professional). He had delivered sessions at various events and conferences in Singapore, Hong Kong, Sri Lanka and India. He has published several articles, tutorials, and game demos on his XNA Game Development Blog – http://uditha.wordpress.com

Table of Contents

01. Introduction

Microsoft .NET platform came long way from its first release. Now lots of Microsoft technologies depend on .NET platform. Technologies like Silverlight, WPF, ASP and WCF among them. In early 2002 there was a technology called **Managed DirectX** (MDX) which used DirectX API. But it mainly uses for small graphic applications. Because of its slow performance. After that Microsoft had reengineered and came up with new technology called XNA. Which was announces March 24, 2004 at Game Developer Conference. Microsoft main goal in XNA was to create a tool set that can target multiple platforms with minimum code change. With the XNA 1.0 release in 2006 they had crate a tool set to support both PC and XBOX360 game development. As of now XNA Supports game development for 4 Platforms with the same C# code. Those are PC, XBOX360, ZUNE and Windows Phone.

Microsoft XNA supports Windows XP, Windows Vista and Windows 7 in PC Game development. And cost of making and selling games on PC is 100% free. All the Visual Studio versions support XNA .Current final release for XNA is 3.1 for Visual Studio 2008.There was XNA 4.0 CTP for Visual Studio 2010 which supports Windows Phone Development. And minimum requirement to run XNA project is having a graphics card that supports DirectX 9.0c and Shader Model 1.1. But for XNA 4.0 CTP you need to have DirectX 10 compatible graphic card.

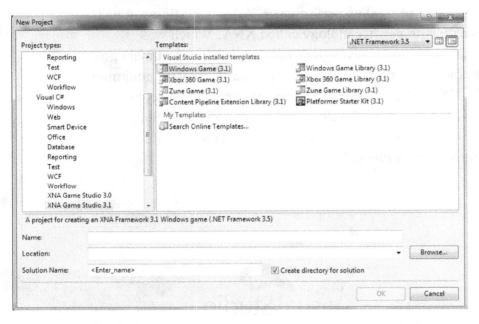

XNA Game Studio 3.1 new Project Template.

XNA Game Studio 4.0 new Project Template.

If you making a Game for XBOX360 and plan to sell it on XBOX Live market Place you need to buy XNA Creators Club premium membership. Which is 99$ per year and it will provide distribution of your game through XBOX Live market place. You can find those games in XBOX360 Game Marketplace under Indie Games Channel.

Now there are over 1000 Indie game available on XBOX Live market place. And all are created using XNA and C#.There are few games on XBOX Live Arcade which created using XNA.

Also new version of the XNA supports Avatars, Xbox live networking, XBOX Live Party API.

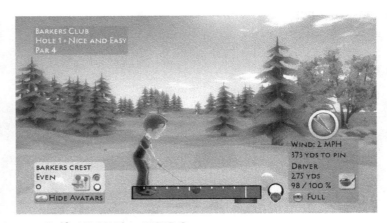

Avatar Golf –XBOX Live INDIE Game.

For the Zune based game development you can use XNA 3.0 or XNA 3.1 .It supports only 2d based games. Because it doesn't have 3d rendering capabilities .With the Zune XNA API you can access ZUNE music player and add the playlists as background music in the

game. Also in Zune HD you can access ZUNE Touch API for XNA.

Windows phone

Windows Phone is earlier named as Windows Mobile. And to make games for windows mobile you need DirectX C++ API. But with the Windows Phone you can use same XNA API to make 2d and 3d games for Windows Phone platform.

XNA API.

Microsoft.Xna.Framework

Microsoft.Xna.Framework.Audio

Microsoft.Xna.Framework.Content

Microsoft.Xna.Framework.Design

Microsoft.Xna.Framework.GamerServices

Microsoft.Xna.Framework.Graphics

Microsoft.Xna.Framework.Input

Microsoft.Xna.Framework.Media

Microsoft.Xna.Framework.Net

Microsoft.Xna.Framework.Storage

02. Hello World in XNA

First create a new Windows Game project.

Start menu->All programs->Microsoft XNA Game studio 3.0 ->Microsoft Visual Studio 2008

->Now you can select New Project from the file menu

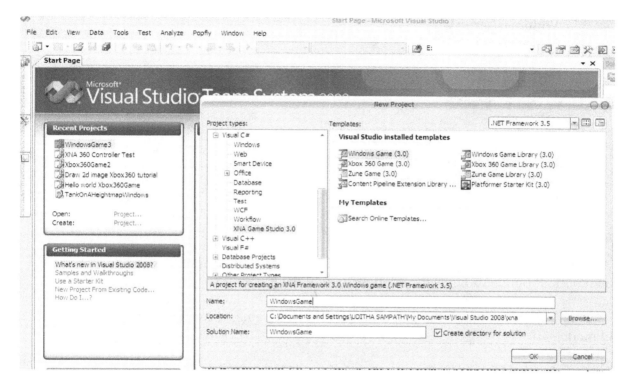

Selecting a New Windows Game project in Visual Studio 2008.

->Then go to XNA game studio 3.0 and select Windows Game (3.0)

In the Solution Explorer you can see two main c# class files, Program.cs and Game1.cs. Program.cs holds the main method of the game.

Content folder contains all the graphic asserts in your game. It can be 2d images, 3d models.

Program.cs

using System;

namespace WindowsGame1

{

static class Program

{

```
/// <summary>

/// The main entry point for the application.

/// </summary>

static void Main(string[] args)

{

using (Game1 game = new Game1())

{

game.Run();

}}}}
```

game.Run() initialize the game class in your application.

Game1.cs file contains important method calls that are unique to XNA. If you're doing Windows from application, you unable to see those type of method calls.

```
using System;

using System.Collections.Generic;

using System.Linq;

using Microsoft.Xna.Framework;

using Microsoft.Xna.Framework.Audio;
```

using Microsoft.Xna.Framework.Content;

using Microsoft.Xna.Framework.GamerServices;

using Microsoft.Xna.Framework.Graphics;

using Microsoft.Xna.Framework.Input;

using Microsoft.Xna.Framework.Media;

using Microsoft.Xna.Framework.Net;

using Microsoft.Xna.Framework.Storage;

In order to work with XNA API ,you need to use Microsoft.Xna.Framework namespaces.That contains Audio,Content, GamerServices, Graphics, Input,

Media,Net,Storage functionalities.

```
public class Game1 :Microsoft.Xna.Framework.Game

{}
```

Our Game1 class is inheriting from the original XNA Framework Game class.

So we can have all the functionalities given in the XNA Framework Game Class.

```
public Game1()
```

```
{
    graphics = new GraphicsDeviceManager(this);

    Content.RootDirectory = "Content";
}
```

this is the constructer of the games. And in this method call graphic device manager gets initialized and Sets the content folder.

```
protected override void Initialize()
{
    // TODO:Add your initialization logic here


    base.Initialize();
}
```

this method is use for initialize the variables ,when the game starts. As an example, if we want to set some default startup location when car game starts.

So we can use this method to do that.

```
protected override void LoadContent()
{
```

```
        // Create a new SpriteBatch, which can be used to draw textures.

        spriteBatch = new SpriteBatch(GraphicsDevice);


        // TODO:use this.Content to load your game content here

    }
```

This method is able to load the graphic content to the VGA card. So we need to specify all the 2d and 3d content in this section.

Example –

```
myfont = Content.Load<SpriteFont>("Arial");


protected override void UnloadContent()
    {
        // TODO:Unload any non ContentManager content here

    }



    protected override void Update(GameTime gameTime)
        {
```

// Allows the game to exit

if (GamePad.GetState(PlayerIndex.One).Buttons.Back == ButtonState.Pressed)

    this.Exit();

// TODO:Add your update logic here

base.Update(gameTime);

}

spriteBatch.DrawString(myfont, "Hello world", new Vector2(10.0f, 10.0f), Color.Black);using System;

This is one of the important methods in the Game class. In a windows form application when you call a certain method as finding the sum, in the GUI you need to click a button or do something similar to that. Then that method gets called once.

But update method is not like that. It will call every 300 ms as a never ending 'for loop'. From that method call, it will detect whether user press any key. Also it used for write logic of the game.

So you need to be careful think when you writing codes in that method.

protected override void Draw(GameTime gameTime)

```
    {

        GraphicsDevice.Clear(Color.CornflowerBlue);

        // TODO:Add your drawing code here

        base.Draw(gameTime);

    }
```

This method is similar as the update method. It also calls in every 300 ms. And this method is using for draw 2d and 3d graphics.

You can do all the 2d and 3d rendering of the game in this method call.

Now I think you know the basic method calls and class structure of a XNA game.

All these codes are automatically generated when you load a windows game project.

Default Game1.cs file

```
using System;

using System.Collections.Generic;

using System.Linq;

using Microsoft.Xna.Framework;
```

```csharp
using Microsoft.Xna.Framework.Audio;

using Microsoft.Xna.Framework.Content;

using Microsoft.Xna.Framework.GamerServices;

using Microsoft.Xna.Framework.Graphics;

using Microsoft.Xna.Framework.Input;

using Microsoft.Xna.Framework.Media;

using Microsoft.Xna.Framework.Net;

using Microsoft.Xna.Framework.Storage;


namespace WindowsGame1
{
    /// <summary>
    /// This is the main type for your game
    /// </summary>
    public class Game1 :Microsoft.Xna.Framework.Game
    {
        GraphicsDeviceManager graphics;

        SpriteBatch spriteBatch;

        SpriteFont myfont;
```

```csharp
public Game1()

{

    graphics = new GraphicsDeviceManager(this);

    Content.RootDirectory = "Content";

}


    /// <summary>

    /// Allows the game to perform any initialization it needs to before starting to run.

    /// This is where it can query for any required services and load any non-graphic

    /// related content. Calling base.Initialize will enumerate through any components

    /// and initialize them as well.

    /// </summary>

    protected override void Initialize()

    {

        // TODO:Add your initialization logic here


        base.Initialize();
```

```csharp
}


/// <summary>
/// LoadContent will be called once per game and is the place to load
/// all of your content.
/// </summary>
protected override void LoadContent()
{
    // Create a new SpriteBatch, which can be used to draw textures.
    spriteBatch = new SpriteBatch(GraphicsDevice);
    myfont = Content.Load<SpriteFont>("Arial");


    // TODO:use this.Content to load your game content here
}


/// <summary>
/// UnloadContent will be called once per game and is the place to unload
/// all content.
/// </summary>
```

```csharp
        protected override void UnloadContent()

        {

            // TODO:Unload any non ContentManager content here

        }



        /// <summary>

        /// Allows the game to run logic such as updating the world,

        /// checking for collisions, gathering input, and playing audio.

        /// </summary>

        /// <param name="gameTime">Provides a snapshot of timing
values.</param>

        protected override void Update(GameTime gameTime)

        {

            // Allows the game to exit

            if (GamePad.GetState(PlayerIndex.One).Buttons.Back ==
ButtonState.Pressed)

                this.Exit();


            // TODO:Add your update logic here
```

```csharp
            base.Update(gameTime);

        }



        /// <summary>

        /// This is called when the game should draw itself.

        /// </summary>

        /// <param name="gameTime">Provides a snapshot of timing
values.</param>

        protected override void Draw(GameTime gameTime)

        {

            GraphicsDevice.Clear(Color.CornflowerBlue);



            // TODO:Add your drawing code here



            base.Draw(gameTime);

        }

    }

}
```

To write a hello world game, first you need to load font to the content folder.

Right click on the content folder and **Add->new item**

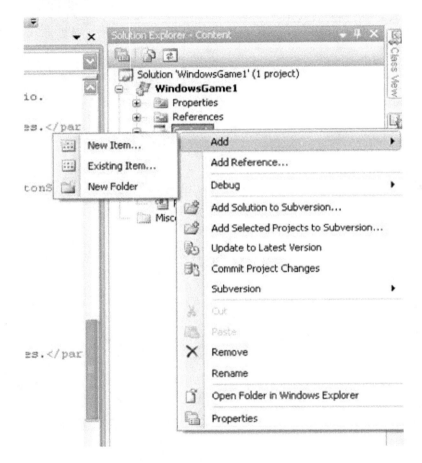

Adding a new item to the Windows Game Project.

And select Sprite font and rename that as **Arial.spritefont**

Arial is the name of the font we are going to use.

You can use any font that install in the Windows font folder.

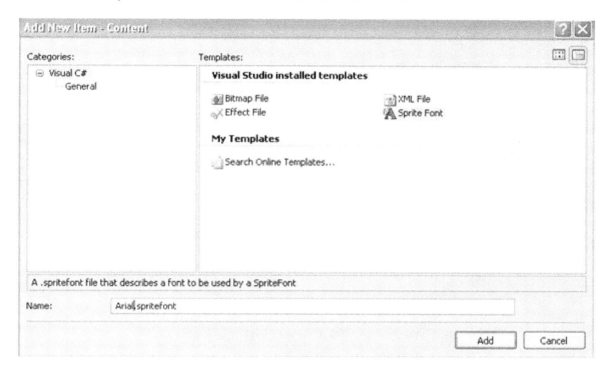

Select Spite Font as the Font file.

Go to **Arial.spritefont** file

if you like you can change the size and style by modifying Size and Style tags.

<Size>14</Size>

<Style>Regular</Style>

Final Arial.spritefont file.

```xml
<?xml version="1.0" encoding="utf-8"?>

<!--

This file contains an xml description of a font, and will be read by the XNA

Framework Content Pipeline. Follow the comments to customize the appearance

of the font in your game, and to change the characters which are available to draw

with.

-->

<XnaContent
xmlns:Graphics="Microsoft.Xna.Framework.Content.Pipeline.Graphics">

<Asset Type="Graphics:FontDescription">


  <!--

  Modify this string to change the font that will be imported.

  -->

  <FontName>Kootenay</FontName>



  <!--
```

Size is a float value, measured in points. Modify this value to change

the size of the font.

-->

<Size>14</Size>

<!--

Spacing is a float value, measured in pixels. Modify this value to change

the amount of spacing in between characters.

-->

<Spacing>0</Spacing>

<!--

UseKerning controls the layout of the font. If this value is true, kerning information

will be used when placing characters.

-->

<UseKerning>true</UseKerning>

<!--

Style controls the style of the font. Valid entries are "Regular", "Bold", "Italic", and "Bold, Italic", and are case sensitive.

-->

<Style>**Regular**</Style>

<!--

If you uncomment this line, the default character will be substituted if you draw

or measure text that contains characters which were not included in the font.

-->

<!-- <DefaultCharacter>*</DefaultCharacter> -->

<!--

CharacterRegions control what letters are available in the font. Every

character from Start to End will be built and made available for drawing. The

default range is from 32, (ASCII space), to 126, ('~'), covering the basic Latin

character set. The characters are ordered according to the Unicode standard.

See the documentation for more information.

-->

<CharacterRegions>

  <CharacterRegion>

```xml
      <Start>span style="color:blue"></Start>

       <End>~</End>

     </CharacterRegion>

    </CharacterRegions>

  </Asset>

 </XnaContent>
```

Now in the Game 1.cs you need to write code to draw a string in the screen. Still we didn`t write any code in our game. Only did the renaming of fonts.

First create an object form SpriteFont to handle our font.

SpriteFont myfont;

Then in the LoadContent() method you can load the font.

myfont = Content.Load<SpriteFont>("Arial");

Then in the Draw() method you can draw the font in the screen.

spriteBatch.Begin();   //start the sprite batch process to draw font

//drawString()method is getting parameters for font type, string valuve,x and y positions in the screen where you need to put the string, and the font color.

//draw the font in the screen

spriteBatch.End();   //end the sprite batch process

Now you can run the project by pressing F5 or by clicking the run button.

Hello World Solution screen shot.

This is the end of the First hello world program.

For this application it only took **5 lines** of code in c#.

But for the unmanaged c++ code to hello world programs it takes about 200 lines of code.

03. 2D Graphics

First you need to load an image to the content folder.

Right click on the content folder and **Add->existing items**

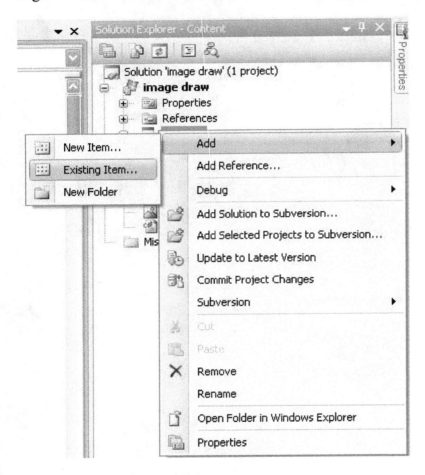

Add existing image file.

And select an image form the hard drive.

It could be .bmp,.png,.jpg ,.dds,.tga

Now in the Game 1.cs you need to write code to draw the image in the screen.

First create an object form Texture2D to handle the image.

Texture2D **mytx;**

Then in the LoadContent() method you can load the image.

mytx = Content.Load<Texture2D>("img");

Then in the Draw() method you can draw the image in the screen.

spriteBatch.Begin(); / /start the sprite batch process to draw font

spriteBatch.Draw(mytx,new Rectangle(100,100,600,400), Color.White);

//Draw() method is getting parameters for texture, rectangle positions which contains x y positions and width and height and finally refresh color of the image.

   spriteBatch.End(); //end the sprite batch process

Now you can run the project by pressing F5 or by clicking the run button.

Draw image on the output.

Final code of Game1.cs

```
using System;

using System.Collections.Generic;

using System.Linq;

using Microsoft.Xna.Framework;

using Microsoft.Xna.Framework.Audio;

using Microsoft.Xna.Framework.Content;

using Microsoft.Xna.Framework.GamerServices;

using Microsoft.Xna.Framework.Graphics;

using Microsoft.Xna.Framework.Input;

using Microsoft.Xna.Framework.Media;

using Microsoft.Xna.Framework.Net;

using Microsoft.Xna.Framework.Storage;

namespace image_draw

{
    /// <summary>
    /// This is the main type for your game
    /// </summary>
```

```csharp
public class Game1 : Microsoft.Xna.Framework.Game

{

GraphicsDeviceManager graphics;

SpriteBatch spriteBatch;

Texture2D mytx;

public Game1()

{

graphics = new GraphicsDeviceManager(this);

Content.RootDirectory = "Content";

}
/// <summary>

/// Allows the game to perform any initialization it needs to before starting to run.

/// This is where it can query for any required services and load any non-graphic

/// related content.  Calling base.Initialize will enumerate through any components

/// and initialize them as well.

/// </summary>

protected override void Initialize()

{
```

```csharp
    // TODO: Add your initialization logic here


    base.Initialize();

}



/// <summary>

/// LoadContent will be called once per game and is the place to load

/// all of your content.

/// </summary>

protected override void LoadContent()

{

// Create a new SpriteBatch, which can be used to draw textures.

spriteBatch = new SpriteBatch(GraphicsDevice);

mytx = Content.Load<Texture2D>("img");




}



/// <summary>
```

```csharp
        /// UnloadContent will be called once per game and is the place to unload

        /// all content.

        /// </summary>

        protected override void UnloadContent()

        {


        }



        /// <summary>

        /// Allows the game to run logic such as updating the world,

        /// checking for collisions, gathering input, and playing audio.

        /// </summary>

        /// <param name="gameTime">Provides a snapshot of timing values.</param>

        protected override void Update(GameTime gameTime)

        {
        // Allows the game to exit

        if (GamePad.GetState(PlayerIndex.One).Buttons.Back == ButtonState.Pressed)

        this.Exit();
```

```csharp
            base.Update(gameTime);

        }


        /// <summary>
        /// This is called when the game should draw itself.
        ///</summary>
        ///<param name="gameTime">Provides a snapshot of timing values.</param>
        protected override void Draw(GameTime gameTime)
        {
            GraphicsDevice.Clear(Color.Black);
            spriteBatch.Begin();
            spriteBatch.Draw(mytx,new Rectangle(100,100,600,400), Color.White);
            spriteBatch.End();
            base.Draw(gameTime);
        }
    }
}
```

Modify the code for 2d animation

Also you can create 2d animation to this example using these lines of codes.

First initialize a float variable to the animation.

```
float val = 0.0f;
```

then in Update() metord increment the valuve to change the position.

```
val = val + 0.3f;
```

finally in the Draw() metord increment the x y positions of the image.

```
spriteBatch.Draw(mytx,new Rectangle(100+(int)val,100+(int)val,600,400),
Color.White);
```

note that we are define a float value and rectangle method is gets int value. So we need to cast float to int.

Then after you press F5 you are ready to play the animation.

04. Using Keyboard and Mouse

First you need to have an image to represent mouse cursor and another image to show the keyboard usage.

You can add those files in to the content folder.

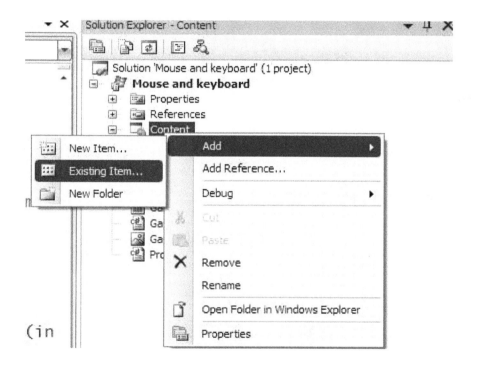

Adds existing image file.

In the Game1.cs file initialize these variables.

```
KeyboardState mykeyboardstate;

//create a keyboardstate  object to get the state of the keyboard



MouseState mymousesatate;

//get the state of the mouse



 SpriteFont myfont;

//add a sprite font to draw String in the screan



Texture2D mytexture, mytexture2;//creating texture object


float Position = 0.0f;//initializing up down position


float Position2 = 0.0f;//initializing left right position


float mousex = 0.0f;//initilizing mousex position


float mousey = 0.0f;//initializing mousey position
```

Now in the LoadContent() metord write code for load the assest.

```
//change the window title
Window.Title = "Using the keyboard+mouse-demo";


myfont = Content.Load<SpriteFont>("Arial");

mytexture = Content.Load<Texture2D>("pic");

mytexture2 = Content.Load<Texture2D>("cursor");
```

Then in the Update() methord you can chack for keyboard and mouse inputs.

```
mykeyboardstate = Keyboard.GetState();//capturing the keybard state


mymousesatate = Mouse.GetState();//capturing mouse state


mousex = (float)mymousesatate.X;//getting the x position of the mouse
```

```csharp
mousey = (float)mymousesatate.Y;//getting the y position of the mouse



// Move 400 pixels each second

  float moveFactorPerSecond = 80 *
(float)gameTime.ElapsedRealTime.TotalMilliseconds / 1000.0f;



//chage the position according to the key pressed up,down,left,right


 if (mykeyboardstate.IsKeyDown(Keys.Up))

     Position -= moveFactorPerSecond;


  if (mykeyboardstate.IsKeyDown(Keys.Down))

      Position += moveFactorPerSecond;




if (mykeyboardstate.IsKeyDown(Keys.Left))

     Position2 -= moveFactorPerSecond;
```

```
if (mykeyboardstate.IsKeyDown(Keys.Right))

        Position2 += moveFactorPerSecond;
```

In the Draw () method you can see the Changes of the inputs by drawing the images.

```
myspitebatch.Begin();//start process


Vector2 position = new Vector2(200.0f + (int)Position2, 200.0f + ((int)Position));
  //setting position with variables (Position1) and (Position2)
  //those variables change the position of the image according to the key pressing


myspitebatch.Draw(mytexture, position, Color.White);//drawing the image


myspitebatch.DrawString(myfont, "Use Arrowkeys to move the image & use
mouse to point", new Vector2(10.0f, 10.0f), Color.Gold);//drawing text on the
screan
```

myspitebatch.Draw(mytexture2, new Vector2(mousex, mousey), Color.White);

    //drawing the cursor image, acording to the mouse position

myspitebatch.End();//end process

Now you can run the project by pressing F5 or by clicking the run button

05. Crating a Menu system

For the Game state you need to add some images to show the user inputs. You can add those files in to the content folder.

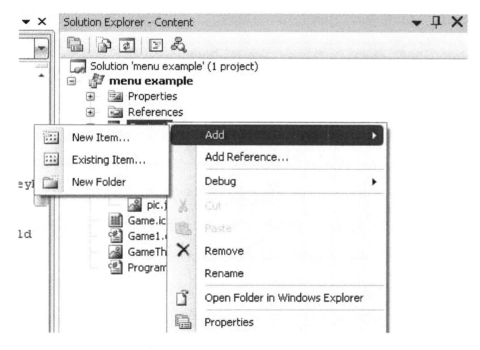

Adds existing image file.

Then you are able to write a code for create a menu system in a XNA game.

In the Game1.cs file initialize these variables.

```
KeyboardState mykeyboardstate;

//create a keyboardstate  object to get the state of the keyboard



 MouseState mymousesatate;//get the state of the mouse


SpriteFont myfont;//add spite batch and spite font as explained in tutorial 01-hello
world


Texture2D mytexture, mytexture2;//creating texture object


float Position = 0.0f;//initializing up down position


float Position2 = 0.0f;//initializing left right position


float mousex = 0.0f;//initilizing mousex position


float mousey = 0.0f;//initilizing mousey position
```

Using enum we can define the different game states.Then we set the initial stage as start state.

```
enum Mygamemode
    {
        start,

        game,

        exit

    } //define game modes start,game,exit


Mygamemode mygame = Mygamemode.start;//assign start mode as initial mode
```

Now in the LoadContent() metord write code for load the assest

```
Window.Title = "Using menu system";
```

```
myspitebatch = new SpriteBatch(graphics.GraphicsDevice);//setting spite batch
for graphic device
```

```
myfont = Content.Load<SpriteFont>("Arial"); //loading font
```

```
mytexture = Content.Load<Texture2D>("pic");//loding image
```

```
mytexture2 = Content.Load<Texture2D>("cursor");//loding cursor image
```

Then in the Update() methord you can chack for keyboard and mouse inputs.

```
mykeyboardstate = Keyboard.GetState();//capturing the state
```

```
mymousesatate = Mouse.GetState();//capturing mouse state
```

```
mousex = (float)mymousesatate.X;//getting the x position of the mouse
```

```
mousey = (float)mymousesatate.Y;//getting the y position of the mouse



// Move 400 pixels each second


float moveFactorPerSecond = 80 *

        (float)gameTime.ElapsedRealTime.TotalMilliseconds / 1000.0f;




//chage the position according to the key pressed up,down,left,right


if (mykeyboardstate.IsKeyDown(Keys.Up))

        Position -= moveFactorPerSecond;




if (mykeyboardstate.IsKeyDown(Keys.Down))

        Position += moveFactorPerSecond;


if (mykeyboardstate.IsKeyDown(Keys.Left))
```

```
        Position2 -= moveFactorPerSecond;
```

```
if (mykeyboardstate.IsKeyDown(Keys.Right))
        Position2 += moveFactorPerSecond;
```

In the Draw () method you can see the Changes by drawing the images.

```
if (mygame == Mygamemode.start) //chack whether you are in the start mode

    {

    myspitebatch.Begin();
```

```
            myspitebatch.DrawString(myfont, "Welcome to the demo ", new Vector2(30.0f,
            30.0f), Color.YellowGreen);


            myspitebatch.DrawString(myfont, "Press Enter to continue..... ", new
            Vector2(30.0f, 80.0f), Color.YellowGreen);

                        myspitebatch.End();




            if (mykeyboardstate.IsKeyDown(Keys.Enter))//chack whather user press enter
            key while he/she in the start mode




            mygame = Mygamemode.game;  //if(true) assign game mode




            }




if (mygame == Mygamemode.game)//chack whether you are in the game mode
```

```
{

        myspitebatch.Begin();//start process




Vector2 position = new Vector2(200.0f + (int)Position2, 200.0f +
((int)Position));




//setting position with variables (Position1) and (Position2)




//those variables change the position of the image according to the key pressing




myspitebatch.Draw(mytexture, position, Color.White);//drawing the image




  myspitebatch.DrawString(myfont, "Use Arrowkeys to move the image & use
mouse to point", new Vector2(10.0f, 10.0f), Color.Gold);//drawing text on the
screan
```

```csharp
myspitebatch.DrawString(myfont, "Use Esc to exit demo", new Vector2(10.0f,
30.0f), Color.Gold);//drawing text on the screan


myspitebatch.Draw(mytexture2, new Vector2(mousex, mousey), Color.White);



//drawing the cursor image, acording to the mouse position
        myspitebatch.End();//end process




if (mykeyboardstate.IsKeyDown(Keys.Escape))//chack whather user press escape
key while he/she in the start mode




mygame = Mygamemode.exit;     //if(true) assign exit mode



}
```

```
if (mygame == Mygamemode.exit) //chack whether you are in the exit mode



{   myspitebatch.Begin();



    myspitebatch.DrawString(myfont, "Goodbuy from the demo ", new
Vector2(30.0f, 30.0f), Color.YellowGreen);



    myspitebatch.DrawString(myfont, "Press Q to exit..... ", new Vector2(30.0f,
80.0f), Color.YellowGreen);



myspitebatch.End();



    if (mykeyboardstate.IsKeyDown(Keys.Q))//chack whather user press enter key
while he/she in the start mode
```

```
    this.Exit();        //if(true) assign game mode

}
```

Now you can run the project by pressing F5 or by clicking the run button.

06. Audio

First you need to add Music files (.mp3, .wav) to the content folder in a new XNA project.

Add existing Audio file.

In the Game1.cs file initialize these variables.

Song **mysong;**//initialize the song

```
SpriteFont myfont;//initialize font

String val;

Texture2D mytx;//initialize texture
```

Now in the LoadContent() metord write code for load the assest

```
Window.AllowUserResizing = true;

//first add new mp3 to a content folder

mysong = Content.Load<Song>("sum41");//load the mp3

myfont = Content.Load<SpriteFont>("Arial");//load the font

mytx = Content.Load<Texture2D>("B");//load the image

MediaPlayer.Play(mysong);//play the song
```

Then in the Update() methord you can write this code segment.

//simple text effect

```
if (gameTime.TotalGameTime.Seconds % 2 == 0)

{
  val = "Playing -sum 41"
}

else

{

  val = "";

}
```

In the Draw () method you can see the Changes by drawing the images.

```
spriteBatch.Begin();  //begin spite batch prosess



spriteBatch.Draw(mytx, new Rectangle(0, 0, Window.ClientBounds.Width,
Window.ClientBounds.Height),

        Color.White);

//draw image



spriteBatch.DrawString(myfont, val,

        new Vector2(30.0f, 30.0f), Color.Orange);

//draw the font
```

spriteBatch.End();//end spite batch process

Now you can run the project by pressing F5 or by clicking the run button.

07. 3D graphics

First you need to have a 3D model. Using software like 3ds max you can create
3d models.

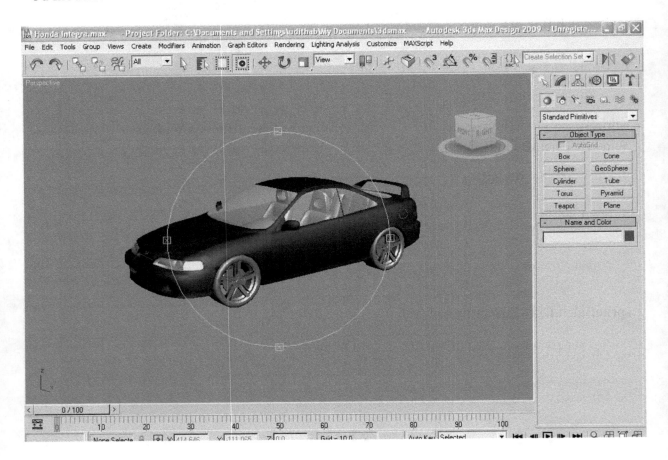

Car 3D model in 3ds max software

Then go to **File->Export** in 3ds max and expoert to a relevent format.

It could be either .x or .fbx

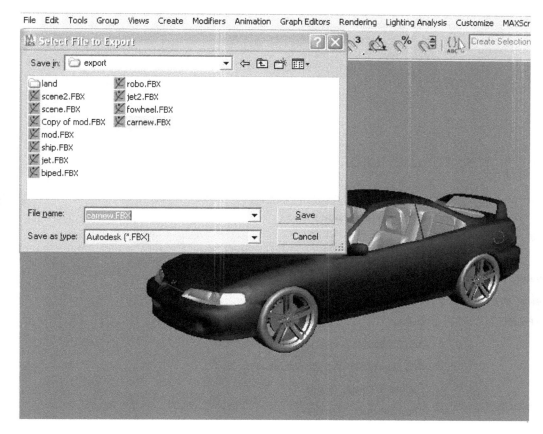

Exporting a 3d model into .FBX format.

Then load that 3D model to the content folder.

Right click on the content folder and **Add->existing items**

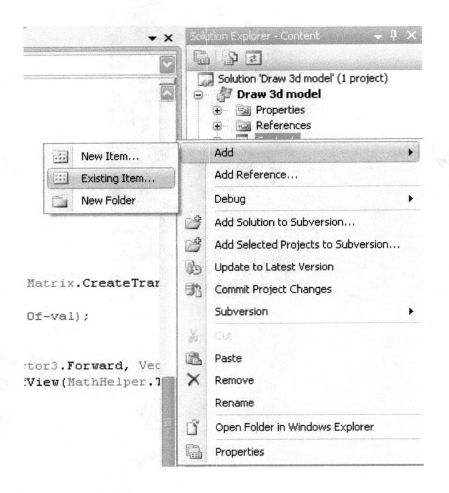

Add the existing 3d model file.

And select that file form the hard drive.

It could be .x and .fbx.

Now in the Game 1.cs you need to write code to draw 3D model in the screen.

First create a object form Model class to handle the model.

Model car;

Then in the LoadContent() method you can load the image.

car = Content.Load<Model>("Car");

then in the Draw() methord you can draw the model in the sceran.

//create a new matrix and copy that tranfomation to 3d model

Matrix[] transforms = new Matrix[car.Bones.Count];

//copy the absolute transforms to the car model.

```csharp
car.CopyAbsoluteBoneTransformsTo(transforms);



//use two foreach loops to loop through the mesh and mesh effect

foreach (ModelMesh mesh in car.Meshes)

{


    foreach (BasicEffect effect in mesh.Effects)



    {


        //enable default lighting provides by XNA.
        effect.EnableDefaultLighting();




        //define the world matrix to locate the position
        effect.World = transforms[mesh.ParentBone.Index] *
Matrix.CreateTranslation(30.0f, -40.0f, -400.0f);




        //define view matrix to set up the camara location
```

```
            effect.View = Matrix.CreateLookAt(Vector3.Zero,
Vector3.Forward, Vector3.Up);




//define projection matrix to model projection ,aspect ratio,

and near and far plane distance.

            effect.Projection =
Matrix.CreatePerspectiveFieldOfView(MathHelper.ToRadians(80.0f), 800.0f
/ 600.0f, 10.0f, 10000.0f);



            }



mesh.Draw(); //Draw the 3d mesh




    }
```

Now
you
can run
the
project
by

pressing F5 or by clicking the run button.

3d Model rendering as the output.

<u>Final code of Game1.cs</u>

```csharp
using System;

using System.Collections.Generic;

using System.Linq;

using Microsoft.Xna.Framework;

using Microsoft.Xna.Framework.Audio;

using Microsoft.Xna.Framework.Content;

using Microsoft.Xna.Framework.GamerServices;

using Microsoft.Xna.Framework.Graphics;

using Microsoft.Xna.Framework.Input;

using Microsoft.Xna.Framework.Media;

using Microsoft.Xna.Framework.Net;

using Microsoft.Xna.Framework.Storage;


namespace Draw_3d_model
{
    /// <summary>
```

/// This is the main type for your game

/// </summary>

```csharp
public class Game1 : Microsoft.Xna.Framework.Game
{

    GraphicsDeviceManager graphics;

    SpriteBatch spriteBatch;

    Model car;


    public Game1()
    {

        graphics = new GraphicsDeviceManager(this);

        Content.RootDirectory = "Content";

    }
```

/// <summary>

/// Allows the game to perform any initialization it needs to before starting to run.

/// This is where it can query for any required services and load any non-graphic

/// related content. Calling base.Initialize will enumerate through any components

/// and initialize them as well.

```csharp
/// </summary>
protected override void Initialize()
{



    base.Initialize();
}


/// <summary>
/// LoadContent will be called once per game and is the place to load
/// all of your content.
/// </summary>
protected override void LoadContent()
{
    // Create a new SpriteBatch, which can be used to draw textures.
    spriteBatch = new SpriteBatch(GraphicsDevice);
    car = Content.Load<Model>("Car");


}


/// <summary>
```

```csharp
/// UnloadContent will be called once per game and is the place to unload
/// all content.
/// </summary>
protected override void UnloadContent()
{


}


/// <summary>
/// Allows the game to run logic such as updating the world,
/// checking for collisions, gathering input, and playing audio.
/// </summary>
/// <param name="gameTime">Provides a snapshot of timing
values.</param>
protected override void Update(GameTime gameTime)
{
    // Allows the game to exit

    if (GamePad.GetState(PlayerIndex.One).Buttons.Back ==
ButtonState.Pressed)

        this.Exit();
```

```csharp
            base.Update(gameTime);

        }


        /// <summary>
        /// This is called when the game should draw itself.
        /// </summary>
        /// <param name="gameTime">Provides a snapshot of timing
values.</param>
        protected override void Draw(GameTime gameTime)
        {
            GraphicsDevice.Clear(Color.Black);


            Matrix[] transforms = new Matrix[car.Bones.Count];
            car.CopyAbsoluteBoneTransformsTo(transforms);


            foreach (ModelMesh mesh in car.Meshes)
            {

                foreach (BasicEffect effect in mesh.Effects)
                {
```

```
        effect.EnableDefaultLighting();


        effect.World = transforms[mesh.ParentBone.Index] *
Matrix.CreateTranslation(30.0f, -40.0f, -400.0f);


        effect.View = Matrix.CreateLookAt(Vector3.Zero, Vector3.Forward,
Vector3.Up);

        effect.Projection =
Matrix.CreatePerspectiveFieldOfView(MathHelper.ToRadians(80.0f), 800.0f /
600.0f, 10.0f, 10000.0f);


      }

    mesh.Draw();



    }


  base.Draw(gameTime);

  }
 }
}
```

Modify the code for 3d animation.

Also you can create a 3d animation to this example using these lines of codes.

First initialize a float variable to the animation.

float **val = 0.0f;**

then in Update() metord increment the value to change the position.

val = val + 0.8f;

finally in the Draw() metord add the val variable to change the position.

effect.World = transforms[mesh.ParentBone.Index] *
Matrix.CreateTranslation(30.0f+val, -40.0f, -400.0f-val);

After that you can press F5 to play the animation.